To My Family

Believe you can and you're halfway there.

– Theodore Roosevelt

First Edition: July 2015

ISBN: 978-0-9905557-4-2

Carla & Liv KIDS™

Available from Amazon.com and other retail outlets.

D1404190

Help for New Students & Parents

From Carla Taylor-Pla, Author • Founder of Carla & Liv KIDS™

Experiencing school and the opportunities it creates is such a rewarding adventure. While attending a new school is exciting and fun, it also can be unnerving for children. Regardless of whether a child has never gone to school, or has attended preschool and is about to enter kindergarten, they share similar concerns: "Will I be all right at school?" and "What will I do there?." All they know is they will be dropped off in a classroom and left by us. Often we leave them with no idea of what to expect.

It's like you or I showing up for a new job without being told our job description!

It's not hard to understand that children, like us, need to know what to expect in order to feel comfortable and excel. That is exactly why I created this book.

After several days of my daughter "Liv" crying when I dropped her off at preschool, a teacher recommended I take photos of the school and discuss them at home with my daughter. I did it the next day, desperate to help Liv feel better. The strategy worked! The crying subsided to a whimper for two days – and then stopped altogether. That's how the idea for **School is New to Me: A Beginner's Guide to Starting School** was born. I spent several years honing this original concept into the current book to help other children meet the challenge of starting school.

School is New to Me: A Beginner's Guide to Starting School shows children what to expect from school – and encourages family discussions about this new experience. The ideas presented in this book have been evaluated by parents, teachers, and my toughest critics -- children. As a result, I've been able to capture what works.

I hope my book will help your child, as it did mine, embrace the new experience of school.

♥ *Carla*

# Why this Book Works

(Patent Pending)

- **<u>Gives children a "game-plan" for school</u>** - This book actually *shows* your child what to expect from school with photos of *real kids* engaged in typical school-like activities. Short descriptions of these activities and interactive exercises help familiarize your little one with school routines.

- **<u>Helps parents prepare their children for school</u>** - The "Parent's Tips" on each page include:
  - ✓ Ideas to help your child start school more at ease and ready to learn;
  - ✓ Recommendations to help you discuss school activities with your child in a manner that gives accurate and positive impressions of school;
  - ✓ Suggestions for fun activities to prepare your little scholar for school.
  *For additional Parent's Tips and information, visit **www.CarlaandLivKids.com**.*

- **<u>Prompts children and parents to discuss school</u>** - Designated pages with a ⟨Let's talk about it.⟩ symbol in the upper left-hand corner provide fun activities that encourage communication about school.

- **<u>Encourages children to share their school experiences</u>** – I created *My School Journal* for your child to express his own school experiences in words and pictures. Use it in combination with **School is New to Me: A Beginner's Guide to Starting School** to help give your child a strong foundation in early learning. Download *My School Journal* from our Web site: **www.CarlaandLivKids.com**. *My School Journal* can be used throughout the year to help build literacy and other skills.

WELCOME TO OUR SCHOOL.

You may be excited and a little nervous about starting school. We were too.

But, we're going to show you that school is a lot of fun.

Parent's Tips

Before the first day of school, take your child on a tour of his new classroom and school to help ease the transition to the new environment. Don't forget to visit the playground too, so your child can associate school with fun and feel more comfortable.

OUR TEACHER

This is my teacher, Ms. Kelley. She is very nice! She answers my questions, teaches me how to do new things, and helps me too.

What is your teacher's name?

Parent's Tips

Try to arrange a time for you and your child to meet her teacher before school starts. Many schools have orientations for parents/caregivers and new students to provide an opportunity to meet teachers and staff.

OUR CLASSROOM

Every morning you'll meet your teacher and other children in your classroom.

OUR CUBBIES

These are our cubbies. There may be a cubby at school with your name on it too. Every morning you will put your things into your cubby, like your backpack, snack and jacket.

Parent's Tips

Help your child pack a backpack or book bag. This will encourage her to get used to preparing for school. Once at school, seeing her name on a cubby will help your child feel welcomed. If her cubby is *outside* of the classroom, it can serve as an effective drop-off point to transition your child from being **with you**, to joining the class **without you**.

Let's talk about it.

What should you put into your cubby at school?

Coat

Lunch Bag

School Folder

My dog, Spot

"SEE YOU LATER, 'ALLIGATOR'."

In the morning, your parent or babysitter will drop you off at school. Don't worry! You'll get picked up when school is over.

Parent's Tips

Many young children initially experience separation anxiety when they're dropped off at school for the first few days or weeks. Assure your child that you (or a designated caregiver) will be back to pick up him/her at the end of the school day. Resist the urge to prolong goodbyes: The sooner you leave, the sooner your child can become engaged in other activities.

FREE PLAY or CHOICE TIME

During free play or choice time, we can choose what to do in the classroom.

Dorothy likes to **d**ress up.

Chris likes to **c**olor with **c**rayons.

We sh**are** and **care** for each other.

Parent's Tips

Play is an essential part of learning. It allows children to satisfy their curiosity by experimenting with things in their physical environment. Play also helps children learn how to cooperate with others through sharing and taking turns. Set aside some time to play with your child and let her lead the activity.

FREE PLAY or CHOICE TIME

Which activity would you like to do during free play or choice time?

 Read a book.

 Pretend to cook.

 Make something new.

 Care for the plant you grew.

Parent's Tips

Discuss the activities on this page with your child: Ask what he would like to do during free play or choice time. This will familiarize your child with some school activities and give him an idea of what to expect in the classroom.

MORNING MEETING or CIRCLE TIME

Your teacher, you and your classmates will talk about what your class will do that day. You might even talk about the weather.

Parent's Tips

During a typical morning meeting or circle time, the teacher might discuss topics like the day's lesson plan, what day of the week it is, or the current weather conditions. This helps children prepare for the day and understand the world around them.

How is the weather today?

Cloudy

Snowing

Sunny

Raining

You will learn new things at school like reading, writing...

...and math.

Parent's Tips

Many classrooms have "learning centers." These are physical areas in the classroom designated for different types of learning through play. Some common learning centers include: reading, arts, and dramatic play (e.g., putting on costumes and pretending to be a doctor, firefighter, etc.).

Sing the alphabet song.

Which letters are missing here?

A, B, C, D, ___, F, G, ___, I,

J, K, L, ___, N, ___, P, Q, R,

___, T, U, ___, W, X, Y, ___

SNACK TIME or LUNCH TIME

If you get hungry, you will eat with your friends...

... in your classroom

in the cafeteria.

Parent's Tips

If you make your child's meal for school, let her help you. Taking an active role in the food preparation will encourage her to eat and enjoy it. Preparing meals also lets children practice following directions, measuring (ingredients) and counting.

Which snacks would you like to bring to school?

Sandwich

Juice

Apple

Something else?

A CLASS TRIP

On special days, we leave our school with our classmates and teacher to visit a fun place like...

... a farm where we pick our own pumpkins

or

... a fire station where we can see how a fire truck works.

Parent's Tips

Class trips can help children understand how what they are learning in school is applied in the "real" world. They also offer an opportunity for you to start a discussion with your child, for example: "What did you see on the trip?"; "What did you do there?"; "What did you like/not like?."

ARTS & CRAFTS

You can use your imagination to make many different kinds of things in arts and crafts.

It's fun to talk about your artwork with your classmates.

Parent's Tips

Make something with your child using crayons, finger paint, or glue (non-toxic) for example. This will encourage him to get engaged in arts and crafts at school. It also can help develop the fine motor skills needed for school.

MUSIC & MOVEMENT

What is your favorite song? Let's sing it!

You're going to have fun singing, dancing,

... and playing instruments at school.

Parent's Tips

Singing nursery rhymes supports language and cognitive development. So go ahead and sing along with your child!

PLAYGROUND or "OUTDOOR PLAY"

We like to play with our friends on the playground. You will make new friends to play with too.

Parent's Tips

Outdoor play is one type of activity that supports gross motor skills, or the ability to use large muscle groups for activities like walking, running, jumping and maintaining balance. Take your child to a playground, preferably the school's, before your child's first day. Continue your visits as your child grows.

Do you see something you would like to play with on the playground?

Tricycle

Monkey bars

Swing

Slide

22

STORY TIME

Your teacher will read books to your class during story time, maybe even one of your favorite books.

My name is Mr. Moo.
I like to go to the zoo.
And if you'd like to listen,
I'll tell you a story or two.
One day I met a wizard,
While walking in a snow blizzard.
"Will this snow disappear?," I asked.
"Can you make these skies clear?," I asked.
"Why yes," he said as he sat,
And he smiled,
And he turned me into...a lizard.

Parent's Tips

Visit your local library. Read any age-appropriate books to your child. This helps develop language and listening skills needed for school and life-long learning. It's never too early to start reading to your child.

GOING HOME

How will you go home...

by car, by bus,

...or another way?

Parent's Tips

Discuss with your child how she will get to and from school (mode of transportation). Address any questions or concerns she has. It also helps to take her to school on the route she will use once school starts.

Bailey's mom is here to pick her up. Your parent or babysitter will pick you up too.

Tomorrow, we will have another great day at school.

What do you think you will like about school?

Parent's Tips

Once school starts, try to stay informed about what your child is doing in class. Feel free to talk to the teachers and ask questions. One way you can encourage your little one to share his school experiences is with **My School Journal**. It's available to download and print at **www.CarlaandLivKids.com**.

Carla Taylor-Pla, Author
Founder, Carla & Liv KIDS™

As a working mother, Carla's daughter is the inspiration for the **School is New to Me** activity book series and the *Carla & Liv KIDS*™ company. Carla has worked to improve educational opportunities for children as a policy advocate for high quality early childhood education. She also served on the leadership team that launched the educational programming brand, PBS KIDS, for **Public Broadcasting Service**. More recently, Carla worked for **The Washington Post** as Manager of Advertising Promotions. She holds a BA from **Yale University**, an M.S. in Journalism from **Northwestern University (Medill School of Journalism)**, and an MBA from **American University**.

Contact Carla Taylor-Pla at:

Carla@CarlaAndLivKids.com

CPSIA information can be obtained at www.ICGtesting.com
Printed in the USA
LVIW01n0811261216
518697LV00012B/55